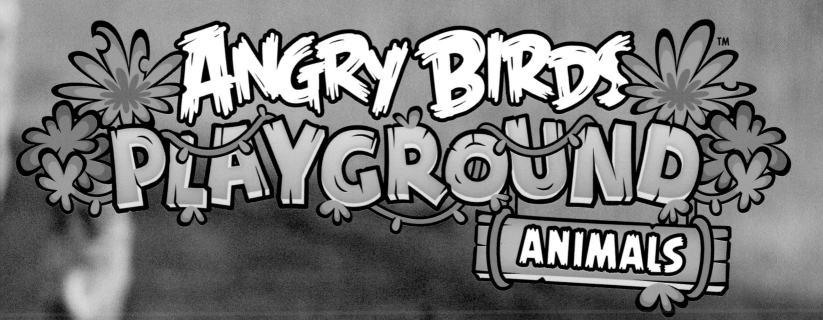

ANGRY BIRDS™
PLAYGROUND
ANIMALS

BY JILL ESBAUM

NATIONAL
GEOGRAPHIC

Washington, D.C.

For Jacob & Joshua — JE

The National Geographic Society is one of the world's largest nonprofit scientific and educational
organizations. Founded in 1888 to "increase and diffuse geographic knowledge," the Society's
mission is to inspire people to care about the planet. It reaches more than 400 million people
worldwide each month through its official journal, *National Geographic,* and other magazines;
National Geographic Channel; television documentaries; music; radio; films; books; DVDs; maps;
exhibitions; live events; school publishing programs; interactive media; and merchandise.
National Geographic has funded more than 10,000 scientific research, conservation and
exploration projects and supports an education program promoting geographic literacy.

For more information, please visit www.nationalgeographic.com,
call 1-800-NGS LINE (647-5463), or write to the following address:
National Geographic Society
1145 17th Street N.W.
Washington, D.C. 20036-4688 U.S.A.

Visit us online at **www.nationalgeographic.com/books**

For librarians and teachers: **www.ngchildrensbooks.org**

More for kids from National Geographic: **kids.nationalgeographic.com**

For information about special discounts for bulk purchases, please contact National Geographic
Books Special Sales: **ngspecsales@ngs.org**

For rights or permissions inquiries, please contact National Geographic Books Subsidiary Rights:
ngbookrights@ngs.org

Hardcover ISBN: 978-1-4263-1266-3
Library Edition ISBN: 978-1-4263-1323-3

Printed in U.S.A.
13/CK-CML/2

Contents

WHERE DID THE PIGS HIDE THE EGGS?

The Angry Birds' eggs have been stolen! The pigs visited five habitats. Could the eggs be in one of those places?

RAIN FOREST

Rain forests are hot and damp, dense with trees, and absolutely teeming with animals, many of which live nowhere else on Earth. Will any of them help the Angry Birds?

HOW WILL WE FIND OUR EGGS? THE EARTH IS A BIG PLACE!

DESERT

Whether hot or cold, deserts get very little precipitation. Yet they are home to more animals than you may think. How will the Angry Birds fare in the hot desert sun?

OCEAN

Five oceans cover more than two-thirds of the Earth. To live here, animals must swim. Wait...can the Angry Birds swim? How will they handle an ocean?

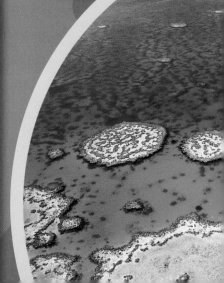

8

SHOULD WE SEARCH SOMEPLACE COLD?

SOMEPLACE HOT?

SOMEPLACE RAINY?

HMM. THE PIGS LIKE WARM, WET PLACES, SO...TO THE RAIN FOREST!

GRASSLAND

You'll know you're in a grassland when you look around and see...grass, of course. Oceans of it. This habitat could be the most relaxing for the Angry Birds. Unless, you know, they run into a hungry lion.

THEY COULD BE ANYWHERE, IN ANY KIND OF HABITAT.

POLAR

Brrr. How will the Angry Birds keep from turning to birdcicles in places that are covered in snow and ice year-round? Do *any* animals live here? You might be surprised.

9

ARE WE THERE YET?

DOES ANYBODY KNOW WHERE WE'RE GOING?

YEAH, I'M TIRED!

OF COURSE! SOUTH AMERICA... HOME TO THE WORLD'S LARGEST RAIN FOREST!

11

WELCOME TO THE RAIN FOREST!

A TROPICAL RAIN FOREST IS HOT AND DAMP. THERE IS SO MUCH RAIN THAT PLANTS GROW VERY CLOSE TOGETHER AND STAY GREEN ALL YEAR.

WOW, THIS PLACE IS HUGE!

HOW WILL WE EVER FIND OUR EGGS?

ASK QUESTIONS! LOOK UNDER EVERY LEAF!

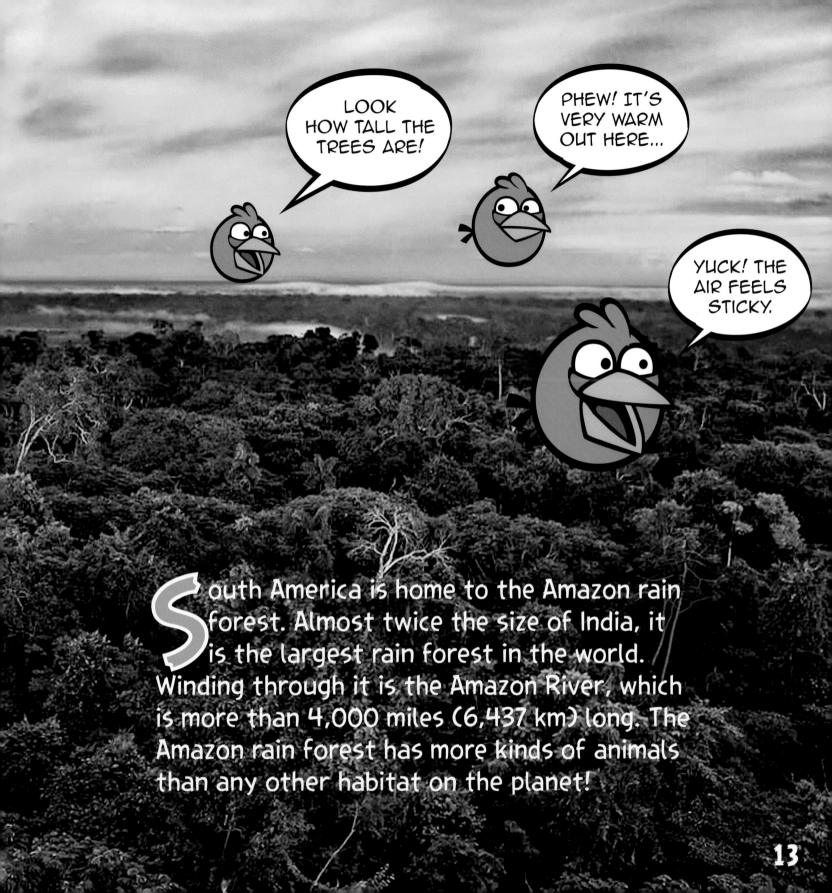

South America is home to the Amazon rain forest. Almost twice the size of India, it is the largest rain forest in the world. Winding through it is the Amazon River, which is more than 4,000 miles (6,437 km) long. The Amazon rain forest has more kinds of animals than any other habitat on the planet!

13

JAGUAR

THIS GUY'S LITTLE, BUT HE MIGHT KNOW SOMETHING.

SIZE: LENGTH: UP TO 6.25 FEET (1.9 M)

ON THE MENU: DEER, RODENTS, REPTILES, MONKEYS, SLOTHS, FISH

SOUNDS LIKE: HAS A DEEP, RUMBLING GROWL

FUN FACT: JAGUARS ARE THE THIRD BIGGEST CATS IN THE WORLD—ONLY LIONS AND TIGERS ARE BIGGER!

Jaguars are mammals that spend their days sleeping and their nights hunting for food. They might appear spotted like a leopard, but if you look closely you'll see that jaguars' spots have smaller spots inside. Even black jaguars, called panthers, have hard-to-see spots!

Jaguar cubs stay with their moms for two years. She teaches them to hunt and protects them from other animals. She also teaches them how to swim. Unlike most cats, jaguars love water! They wade right in to fish, take baths, or splash playfully.

MR. JAGUAR, SIR, HAVE YOU SEEN OUR EGGS?

HARPY EAGLE

RAIN FOREST

MY FEATHERS LOOKED LIKE THAT ONCE.

16

YOU MEAN THAT TIME YOU RAN INTO THE BUG ZAPPER?

Harpy eagles are easy to identify—when alert or upset, their head feathers pop straight up. Patient hunters, a harpy can sit on a branch all day, watching for a small animal to pass by below. When it does, this speedy bird zooms down, snatches its prey with powerful claws, and twists and turns back up through the trees to its nest.

Nests are built of sticks, leaves, and animal fur. They're so big that YOU could take a comfy nap there.

Once an egg hatches, both parents hunt to feed their hungry chick. Even after it is grown, a chick often drops in at Mom and Dad's for an easy meal.

SIZE: HEIGHT: 35-41 INCHES (89-104 CM), WINGSPAN 6-7 FEET (1.8-2.5 M)

ON THE MENU: SLOTHS, MONKEYS, OPOSSUMS, REPTILES, BIRDS

SOUNDS LIKE: USUALLY QUIET, BUT SOMETIMES WILL CROAK, WHISTLE, OR CLICK

FUN FACT: HARPY EAGLES WILL REUSE THE SAME NEST FOR YEARS!

SCHNEIDER'S DWARF CAIMAN

SIZE: LENGTH: 5.5–7.5 FEET (1.7–2.3 M)

ON THE MENU: FISH, SNAKES, CAPYBARAS AND OTHER MAMMALS

SOUNDS LIKE: HISSES, HUFFS, GRUNTS, BARKS, AND ROARS

FUN FACT: CAIMANS MIGHT ACT TOUGH, BUT THEY ARE A JAGUAR'S FAVORITE SNACK!

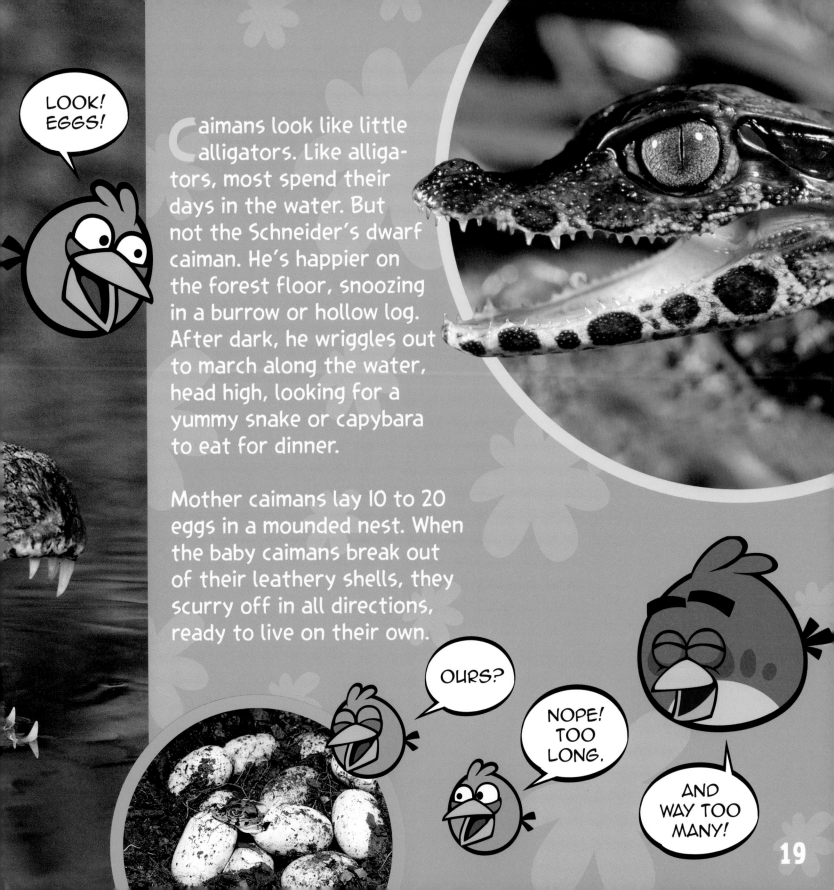

LOOK! EGGS!

Caimans look like little alligators. Like alligators, most spend their days in the water. But not the Schneider's dwarf caiman. He's happier on the forest floor, snoozing in a burrow or hollow log. After dark, he wriggles out to march along the water, head high, looking for a yummy snake or capybara to eat for dinner.

Mother caimans lay 10 to 20 eggs in a mounded nest. When the baby caimans break out of their leathery shells, they scurry off in all directions, ready to live on their own.

OURS?

NOPE! TOO LONG.

AND WAY TOO MANY!

19

POISON DART FROG

Poison dart frogs may be bright and beautiful, but watch out! Those fancy colors are a warning. They tell other animals: Stay away. I'm poisonous! Despite their tiny size, these frightening frogs are among the deadliest animals in the world.

Like all amphibians, poison dart frog babies hatch from eggs. The mother frog lays the eggs on a tiny leaf, and then the father frog takes over. He eggsits, careful to keep them from drying out. After hatching, some of the tiny tadpoles swim onto their father's back and stick like glue. He carries them to a safe, watery place, where they are left on their own to grow.

DON'T EAT US!

WE'RE POISONOUS TOO!

NO WE'RE NOT!

20

SIZE: LENGTH: 1–2.5 INCHES (2.5–6.35 CM)

ON THE MENU: ANTS, TERMITES, SPIDERS, AND OTHER TINY BUGS

SOUNDS LIKE: MALES MAKE A HIGH-PITCHED PEEP TO ATTRACT FEMALES

FUN FACT: A GOLDEN POISON DART FROG HAS ENOUGH POISON TO KILL 20,000 MICE.

SLOTH

RAIN FOREST

HE SAYS THE ANACONDA MIGHT KNOW ABOUT OUR EGGS.

Sloths are the world's slowest-moving mammals—so slow that tiny green plants called algae grow on their fur, making it look green. Sloths have long, strong claws that help them hold branches tightly. That's good, because they do tons of stuff while hanging upside down. Eating. Sleeping. Even having babies. When a baby sloth is born, the first thing it has to do is grab on to its mother's hair to keep from falling!

On the ground, sloths' back legs are weak. So sloths dig in with their front claws and pull themselves forward, bellies dragging. They are excellent swimmers, though, unafraid to drop from a branch into the water. *SPLASH!*

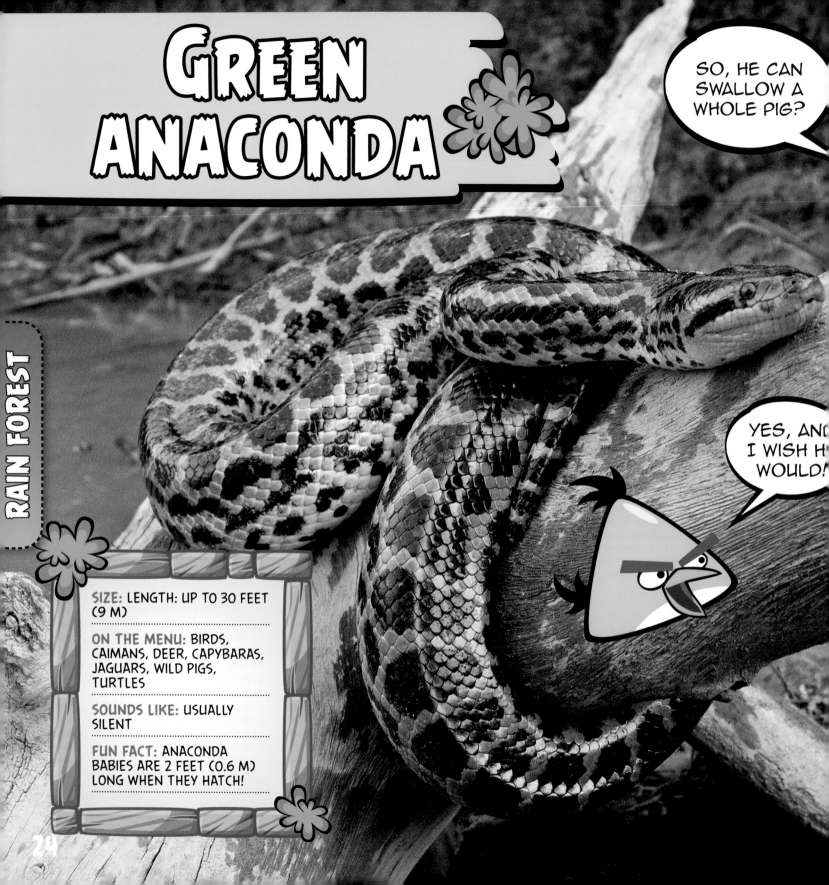

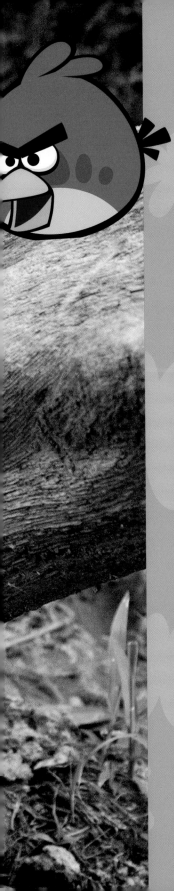

Green anacondas weigh more than any snake in the world. They are the widest, too. Their eyes and nose are on top of their heads, so they can lie in the water almost completely covered. Then—surprise!—they sneak up on their prey. They quickly curl their powerful bodies around an animal, squeezing until it can no longer breathe. Their jaws are not connected at the sides, so they can stretch w–i–d–e to swallow prey whole, no matter how big.

Mother anacondas have two to three dozen baby snakes at one time. The babies are longer than your arm when they hatch and slither off right away to begin swimming and hunting.

GULP. I'M NOT ASKING HIM ABOUT OUR EGGS!

ME NEITHER!

NOT IT!

25

BLACK-HANDED SPIDER MONKEY

These monkeys live high in rain forest trees. They use their muscular tails like an extra hand to climb, reach for fruit, or swing from branches.

A baby sticks close to its mother, often clinging to her back. By the time a monkey is two years old, the free rides are over. It scampers off with friends to explore or play, jumping and rolling around on one another. But if a jaguar or other enemy gets too close, their fun stops. The monkeys try to frighten the animal away by making scary faces, shaking limbs, and barking. If none of that works, there's one thing left to do: FLEE!

SIZE: LENGTH: UP TO 14-26 INCHES (35-66 CM)

ON THE MENU: FRUIT, SEEDS, NUTS, LEAVES, INSECTS, BIRD EGGS

SOUNDS LIKE: SNORTS, CHUFFS, BARKS, SCREECHES

FUN FACT: FROM BELOW, THESE LITTLE MONKEYS LOOK LIKE SPIDERS!

BLUE MORPHO BUTTERFLY

THE BLUE MORPHO SAYS SHE REMEMBERS SEEING THE PIGS!

WHERE?

RAIN FOREST

28

THE DESERT.

C'MON, BIRDS, LET'S GO!

SIZE: WIDTH: 5-8 INCHES (12.7-20.3 CM), WINGSPAN: 3-6 INCHES (8-15 CM)

ON THE MENU: CATERPILLAR STAGE: LEAVES; BUTTERFLY STAGE: JUICE OF ROTTED FRUIT

SOUNDS LIKE: SILENT

FUN FACT: THE BLUE MORPHO TASTES ROTTING FRUIT WITH SPECIAL SENSORS ON ITS LEGS.

Blue Morpho butterfly eggs stick to a leaf like tiny green balloons. In time, caterpillars crawl from the eggs and hungrily *chomp, chomp, chomp.* Don't bother them while they're eating, though. If you do, they give off a stinky smell to make you go away. *Phew!*

After some time, each caterpillar wraps itself in a protective cover called a chrysalis. The chrysalis hangs, still and silent. Inside, an amazing change is taking place—the caterpillar is turning into a butterfly. After crawling out, the new butterfly waits patiently for its wings to dry. Then it flits away, flashing brown-blue, brown-blue in the sunlight.

29

WELCOME TO THE DESERT!

A DESERT IS DRY AND WINDY. MOST ARE HOT. EVEN WITH ITS ROCKY, SANDY SOIL, THE DESERT IS HOME TO MANY ANIMALS.

DESERT

The Mojave, one of the world's smaller deserts (about 25,000 sq mi/64,750 sq km), is located in the southwestern United States. Within its borders is Badwater Basin, the lowest place in North America, and also one of the hottest and driest.

33

TOWNSEND'S BIG-EARED BAT

DESERT

SIZE: WINGSPAN: ABOUT ONE FOOT (0.3 M)

ON THE MENU: MOSTLY MOTHS

SOUNDS LIKE: COMMUNICATES WITH CLICKS

FUN FACT: THIS BAT CAN HOVER LIKE A HELICOPTER TO TAKE A DRINK OF WATER.

WHY IS SHE HANGING UPSIDE DOWN?

MAYBE SHE'S EXERCISING.

Bats make sounds as they swoop through the night sky—sounds too high for a human to hear. Sound waves bounce off objects and back to the bat, helping the bats to understand their location. This process, called echolocation, makes it easy for the bats to find the flying insects they like to eat.

Bats spend more than half of the year hibernating. They usually can be found in tucked-away spots, like caves or under bridges. To help protect them- selves, bats sleep hanging upside down, ready to fly off in a quick escape.

35

GREATER ROADRUNNER

HEY, BUDDY, SEEN ANY NEW EGGS AROUND HERE?

SIZE: HEIGHT: ABOUT 2 FEET (0.6 M)

ON THE MENU: INSECTS, LIZARDS, SMALL RODENTS, SNAKES, OR WHATEVER THEY CAN CATCH

SOUNDS LIKE: COOS, WHIRRING; FEMALES SOMETIMES REPEAT A SHARP BARK

FUN FACT: A ROADRUNNER'S FEET HAVE TWO TOES POINTING AHEAD AND TWO TOES POINTING BACK.

Roadrunners are members of the cuckoo family. They can fly, but would rather stay on the ground, zipping after the insects, lizards, and snakes they like to eat. Long tails help these speedy birds keep their balance.

Roadrunners build their nests low in cacti or other desert trees.

To warm up on cool mornings, a roadrunner stands still, its feathers fluffed out so the sun's heat can reach its skin. *Ahhh.*

Gila monsters live in underground burrows. They only come out to warm up in the sunshine and to hunt. Gilas are venomous. Venom is poison that comes out through grooves in their teeth when they bite another animal. They have poor eyesight, so they find dinner by smelling the air and even tasting it by flicking their forked tongues.

Gila eggs are large and leathery.

ARE THOSE OUR EGGS?

NOPE, WRONG SHAPE.

TARANTULA

Tarantulas are hairy, eight-eyed spiders. Insects are their favorite food, but they'll also go after frogs, toads, and mice. They don't capture prey in a web like some spiders, but instead wait quietly inside their burrow for, say, an unlucky beetle to happen by... When one does, the tarantula grabs it.

A spider can't eat solid food, so how does it eat a captured insect? The spider injects a special fluid into its victim that turns the body into juice. Then the spider sucks it up through its straw-like mouth.

Baby tarantulas are born with 500 to 1,000 brothers and sisters.

DESERT

1,000 BABY TARANTULAS?

AWK!

YUCK!

LET'S GET OUTTA HERE!

SIZE: BODY: 2-3 INCHES (5-7.5 CM) WIDE, LEGS: 4 INCHES (10 CM) LONG

ON THE MENU: BEETLES, CATERPILLARS, CRICKETS, GRASSHOPPERS, FROGS, TOADS, MICE, SMALL LIZARDS

SOUNDS LIKE: SILENT

FUN FACT: WHEN IT'S IN DANGER, A TARANTULA RUBS HAIRS OFF ITS ABDO-MEN AND BRUSHES THEM INTO AN ENEMY'S EYES.

41

BLACK-TAILED JACKRABBIT

DESERT

QUICK! ASK HIM IF HE'S SEEN...

HE'S A FUZZY LITTLE GUY.

I STILL THINK I'M CUTER!

This "rabbit" is actually a hare. What's the difference? Rabbits are born hairless, their ears and eyes closed. Hares are born with all their fur, eyes open. Even the bottoms of a jackrabbit's feet are furry. This keeps the feet cooler and makes the hard ground feel softer.

A jackrabbit flashes its tail to warn others of danger. When chased by a coyote, badger, or other predator, a jackrabbit zigzags away *fast*.

TOO LATE. HE'S GONE.

SIZE: HEIGHT: UP TO 2 FEET (0.6 M), WEIGHT: 3-9 POUNDS (1.4-4 KG)

ON THE MENU: CACTI, FLOWERING PLANTS, GRASS, LEAVES, SHRUBS, TWIGS

SOUNDS LIKE: SCREECHING CRIES WHEN UPSET

FUN FACT: JACKRABBITS CAN SWIM.

DESERT HORNED LIZARD

SIZE: LENGTH: UP TO 5.5 INCHES (14 CM)

ON THE MENU: ANTS

SOUNDS LIKE: HISSES WHEN THREATENED

FUN FACT: DESERT HORNED LIZARDS DON'T NEED TO DRINK WATER. THEY GET ALL THE MOISTURE THEIR BODIES NEED FROM THE ANTS THEY EAT.

HIS BELLY IS FULL OF ANTS!

A desert horned lizard can't get enough of ants, its favorite food. It will sit still and let ants crawl all over it before—*snap! snap! snap!*—gobbling them down.

When a predator nears, this lizard hides. If caught in the open, it shuffles sideways to bury itself in the sand, or flattens itself and lies perfectly still, hoping nobody sees it. If caught, it hisses and puffs up like a spiky balloon.

EW, ANT BREATH.

BURROWING OWL

These small, long-legged owls live in burrows dug by ground squirrels or badgers. They have plenty of ways to catch a meal. They can run on the ground after beetles, catch bats on the fly, or swoop down from the sky to snatch ground squirrels.

Baby owls, called owlets, are born in nesting burrows. Their mothers stay with them at all times, while their fathers hunt to keep everyone fed.

Four weeks after hatching, owlets leave the burrow to begin chasing insects.

THEY LOOK ANGRY.

DESERT

CALIFORNIA KING SNAKE

DESERT

SIZE: LENGTH: ADULTS 2.5–3.5 FEET (0.8–1.1 M), BABIES: 12 INCHES (30 CM)

ON THE MENU: LIZARDS, RODENTS, TURTLE EGGS, FROGS, BIRDS AND THEIR EGGS AND CHICKS, OTHER SNAKES

SOUNDS LIKE: HISSES

FUN FACT: CALIFORNIA KING SNAKES EAT THEIR VICTIMS HEAD FIRST. WHY? THE VICTIM'S SLIPPERY SALIVA MAKES THE REST OF ITS BODY EASIER TO SWALLOW.

OUR EGGS! OUR EGGS!

AND THEY'RE HATCHING! COME TO PAPA!

WAIT. DID OUR EGGS HAVE SNAKES INSIDE?

When this snake is hungry, its bird and lizard neighbors aren't the only ones that should be careful. King snakes will eat other snakes! Even venomous rattlers are no match. The king simply wraps itself around its victim and squeezes until the victim cannot breathe. Then, down the hatch!

There are many different species of king snakes. These snakes can feel vibrations in the ground, so they know when other animals are approaching. Luckily for their prey, king snakes can't see very well, so if an animal stands still, the snake might just slither on by.

Baby snakes hatch 45 to 60 days after their mother lays them.

NOPE. NOT OURS. GO, BIRDS, GO!

49

WELCOME TO THE OCEAN!

SALTWATER OCEANS COVER MORE THAN TWO-THIRDS OF THE EARTH AND ARE HOME TO TENS OF THOUSANDS OF PLANT AND ANIMAL SPECIES.

THIS WILL TAKE FOREVER.

WHERE DO WE BEGIN SEARCHING?

I'M TIRED ALREADY.

52

The Pacific, covering 65.4 million square miles (169.5 million sq km), is the largest of the world's oceans. It covers one-third of the Earth, stretching from the Arctic in the north all the way south to the continent of Antarctica. It bumps into Asia and Australia and laps at the coasts of North America and South America.

HUMPBACK WHALE

OCEAN

54

ME, TOO! BLUB-BLUB-BOP-BOP.

WHY ARE YOU ALL TALKING ROBOT?

Humpbacks travel in groups called pods. They spend part of the year in warm, tropical waters, then swim north to spend summer in a cooler part of the ocean. Humpbacks are huge, but acrobatic. They can shoot out of the water, then splash back down, sometimes after a graceful twirl.

Humpback whales are famous for their singing. Their songs are filled with *bloops*, long *ahhs*, moans, cries, and grunts.

A whale calf is born in warm, shallow water. Just after, its mother uses a flipper to push the 2.5-ton (2.3-metric ton) calf up to the surface to take its first breath of air.

SIZE: LENGTH: 48–62.5 FEET (14.6–19 M), WEIGHT: 79,000 POUNDS (36 METRIC TONS), TAIL FLUKE: UP TO 12 FEET (3.7 M) WIDE

ON THE MENU: KRILL, PLANKTON, SMALL FISH

SOUNDS LIKE: FAMOUS FOR THEIR COMPLICATED SONGS, WHICH CAN GO ON FOR HOURS

FUN FACT: HUMPBACKS HAVE WHITE PATTERNS UNDER THEIR TAIL FIN, OR FLUKE. EACH WHALE'S FLUKE PATTERN IS DIFFERENT.

SEA OTTER

OCEAN

LOOKS COMFY.

BUT WHERE IS HIS FLOATY TUBE?

WE CAN'T SWIM LIKE THAT. WHAT WILL WE DO?

I'VE GOT AN IDEA...

56

Sea otters spend much of their lives floating on their backs. They even sleep on their backs, wrapping themselves in long blades of kelp to stay in one place. Otter mothers have their babies while floating, too. The pups and their mothers spend lots of time cuddling as they rock atop the waves.

A sea otter's skin stays dry. How is that possible? It has two layers of fur: the layer you see and another, fluffier under-layer that traps air and warmth next to the otter's skin.

Sea otters use rocks as tools to break open the shells of the clams and mussels they like to eat.

HAS SHE SEEN ANY PIGS?

NOPE. LET'S DIVE. MAYBE WE'LL HAVE BETTER LUCK UNDERWATER.

GIANT PACIFIC OCTOPUS

OCEAN

SIZE: ARM LENGTH: 9.75–16 FEET (3–5 M), WEIGHT: 22–110 POUNDS (10–50 KG), BUT MAY GROW MUCH LARGER

ON THE MENU: CRABS, OYSTERS, CLAMS, MUSSELS, SCALLOPS, SHRIMP, FISH, SHARKS

SOUNDS LIKE: SILENT

FUN FACT: NEWBORN OCTOPUSES ARE NO BIGGER THAN A GRAIN OF RICE.

GREAT IDEA, BLUE. THIS SCUBA GEAR IS PERFECT FOR SWIMMING UNDERWATER.

YIKES! HE'S GONNA CATCH US! SWIM FASTER!

Giant Pacific octopuses are the largest in the world. They are very good hiders and are hard to capture alive, so nobody knows exactly how big they can grow. To hunt, these giants stretch out their sensitive, suckered arms to feel along the ocean floor or into cracks in rocks. If they find a crab, they bite it open with their tough beak to get at the tasty meat inside.

Octopuses are shy. They can change their skin color in an instant, blending with sand or rocks. This makes them hard to see and protects them from enemies. If an enemy gets too close, an octopus hides itself by squirting a cloud of purple-black ink, then hurries to its den.

HAWAIIAN MONK SEAL

Hawaiian monk seals are found in only one place on Earth: the Hawaiian Islands chain. So few of these seals are left that they soon could disappear forever.

Late every summer and into the fall, adult seals shed their old skin and hair. This does not hurt the seals, and the new hair that grows helps them stay warm when winter brings cooler water temperatures.

Pups are born near shallow water. Their mothers keep a close eye on them for their first weeks, not even leaving them to eat.

ISN'T THAT SAND HOT? EECH! OOCH! OUCH!

60

61

GREAT HAMMER-HEAD SHARK

HIS EYES ARE ON OPPOSITE SIDES OF HIS HEAD!

Great hammerheads are the largest of the nine kinds of hammerhead sharks. Their eyes are on the outside of their wide, rectangular heads. This makes it easy to see all around themselves. Other extra-sharp senses help them find their favorite prey—stingrays—even when the rays are buried in the sand and impossible to see!

During the summer, hammerheads migrate north in large groups, looking for cooler waters.

COOL! BUT...WHAT HAPPENS IF HE NEEDS GLASSES?

62

I'M PRETTY SURE THAT'S MORE EGGS THAN WE HAD.

NOPE, NOT OURS.

Clownfish are always found living with sea anemones—always. That's because the two animals need each other. The anemone's stinging tentacles will kill most fish—but not the clownfish. So these colorful little nibblers dart in and out, keeping the anemone free of algae and harmful parasites. And the anemone repays the favor. Its poisonous tentacles give the fish a safe place to hide when predators come around!

Newly hatched clownfish drift high in the water for a week or two. When the fish are about a half inch long, they swim down, down, down to find an anemone home.

SIZE: LENGTH: UP TO 5 INCHES (13 CM)

ON THE MENU: ALGAE, PLANKTON AND OTHER TINY CREATURES, FISH REMAINS

SOUNDS LIKE: SILENT

FUN FACT: A CLOWNFISH STAYS WITH THE SAME ANEMONE ITS ENTIRE LIFE, NEVER SWIMMING MORE THAN A FEW FEET AWAY.

RED-FOOTED BOOBY

A red-footed booby spends much of its life far from land, soaring above the waves. When it spies a yummy fish or squid, it wraps its long wings around itself and dives straight into the ocean to chase the meal!

Red-footed boobies build stick nests in shrubs. Parents take turns using their feet to keep their only egg warm.

YEAH, NOW LET'S KEEP LOOKING!

THOSE SNORKELS REALLY HELPED!

SIZE: LENGTH: 2.1–2.5 FEET (0.6–0.8 M), WINGSPAN: 3–3.3 FEET (0.9–1 M)

ON THE MENU: FLYING FISH, SQUID

SOUNDS LIKE: *AAWKS*, SCREECHY SQUAWKS

FUN FACT: RED-FOOTED BOOBIES HAVE NOSTRILS THAT CLOSE WHEN THEY DIVE AND WEBBED FEET THAT HELP THEM SWIM.

LEATHERBACK SEA TURTLE

RIGHT. BESIDES, WE DIDN'T HAVE THAT MANY EGGS!

HEY! COULD THOSE BE OUR EGGS? THEY'RE THE RIGHT COLOR.

SHE JUST PUT THOSE IN THERE. YOU SAW IT.

SIZE: LENGTH: UP TO 7 FEET (2 M), WEIGHT: UP TO 2,000 POUNDS (900 KG)

ON THE MENU: MOSTLY JELLYFISH, PLUS OTHER SMALL PREY

SOUNDS LIKE: GRUNTS (POSSIBLY)

FUN FACT: THE FEMALE IS ABOUT 16 YEARS OLD BEFORE SHE'S READY TO LAY EGGS. TO DO THAT, EVEN AFTER ALL THOSE LONG YEARS AT SEA, SHE FINDS HER WAY BACK TO THE VERY BEACH WHERE SHE HERSELF WAS HATCHED.

Sea turtles have been on Earth since the time of dinosaurs. And leatherbacks are the largest kind. They swim farther and dive deeper than any other turtle. Their front flippers are longer and more powerful than those of their turtle cousins, too.

Other turtles have hard shells. But not the leatherback. Its thick shell is tough and feels—you guessed it—leathery.

A male leatherback spends all of his life at sea. A female comes ashore every two or three years. She digs a deep hole in the sand and lays 60 to 100 eggs. She does this again and again during the breeding season. Then she swims away, and the eggs are left alone. Hatchlings dig out of the sand with one thought in their heads: Get me to the ocean!

A FRIEND OF THAT TURTLE SUGGESTED LOOKING IN THE GRASSLANDS OF TASMANIA.

OR MAYBE IT WAS TANZANIA. NOW I CAN'T REMEMBER.

WE'LL HAVE TO SPLIT UP! BLUES, YOU TAKE TANZANIA. WE'LL HEAD OFF TO TASMANIA AND MEET UP WITH YOU LATER.

AWK!

AND BE CAREFUL, GUYS. DON'T DO ANYTHING DANGEROUS!

69

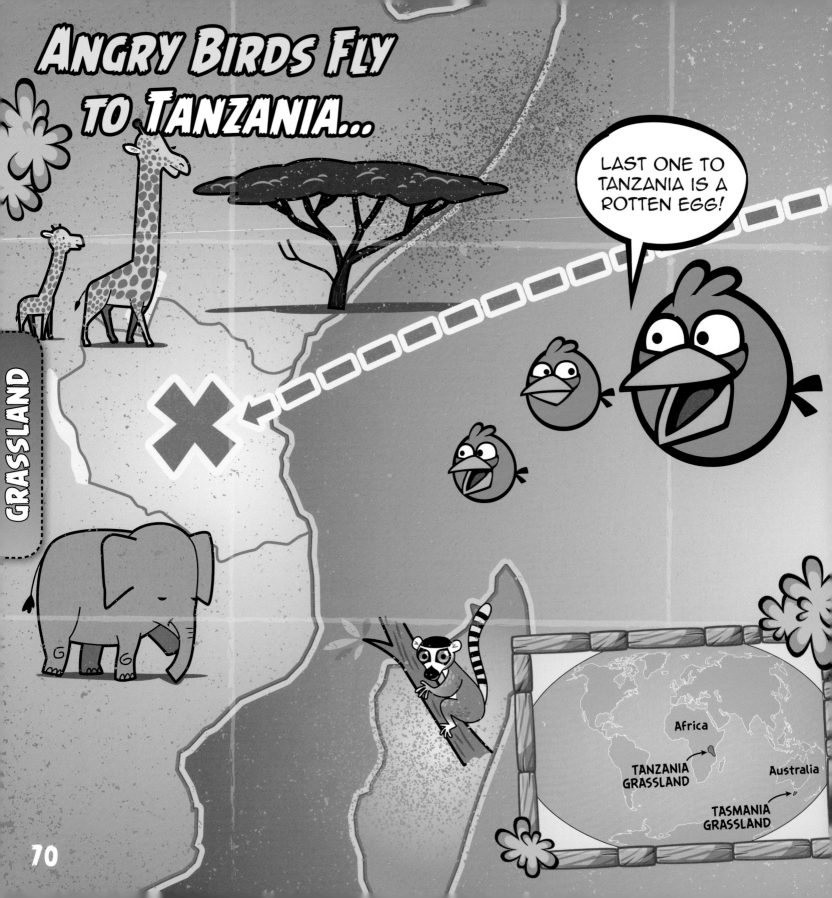

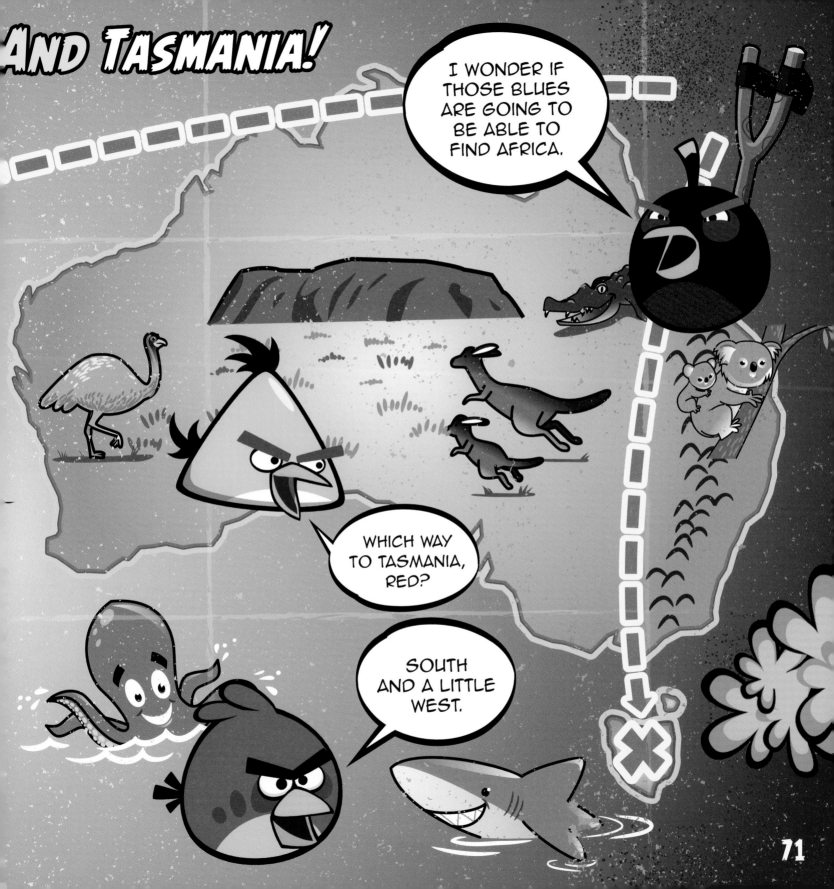

WELCOME TO THE GRASSLAND!

A GRASSLAND IS A SEA OF GRASS, OFTEN GROWING BETWEEN DESERTS AND FORESTS. LOTS OF GRASSES AND SHRUBS GROW HERE, BUT NOT MANY TREES.

HERE WE ARE! TASMANIA!

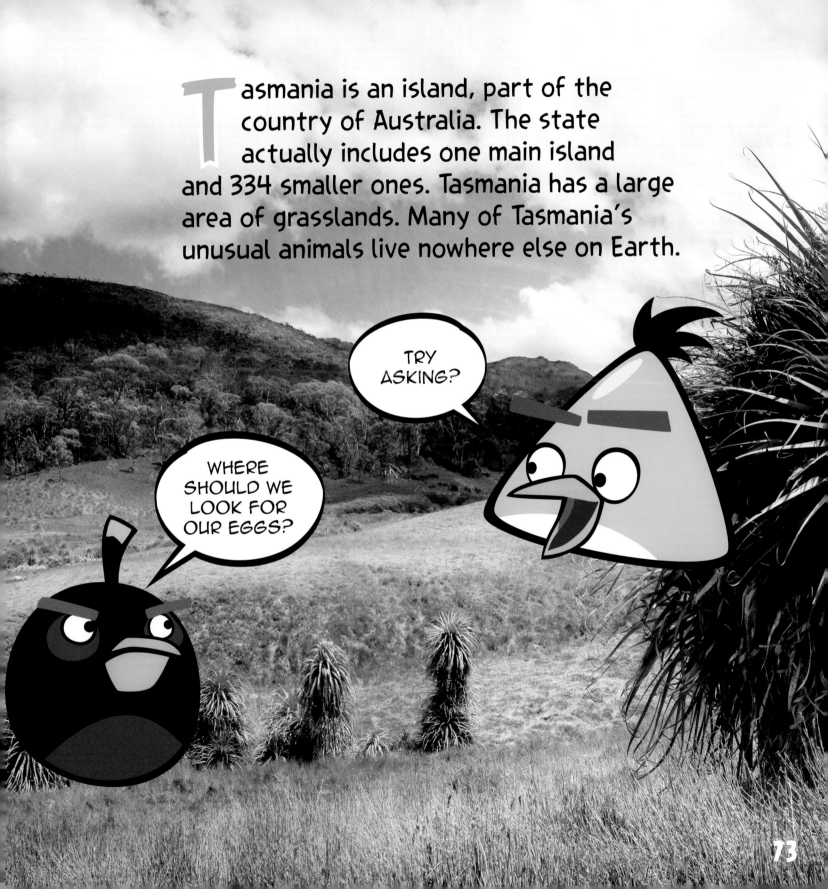

Tasmania is an island, part of the country of Australia. The state actually includes one main island and 334 smaller ones. Tasmania has a large area of grasslands. Many of Tasmania's unusual animals live nowhere else on Earth.

RED-NECKED WALLABY

HEY, MAYBE OUR EGGS ARE IN THAT POUCH.

SIZE: HEIGHT: UP TO 3.4 FEET (1 M), NOT COUNTING THE TAIL, WEIGHT: UP TO 60 LBS (27 KG)

ON THE MENU: GRASSES AND HERBS

SOUNDS LIKE: CLUCKS, COUGHS, HISSES, SOFT GROWLS

FUN FACT: SOMETIMES WALLABY MOTHERS HAVE TO DO A LITTLE POUCH CLEANING. WITH JOEYS DOING *EVERYTHING* IN THERE, IT GETS A LITTLE STINKY.

Wallabies are marsupials. That means their babies, called joeys, are born teeny tiny and have to climb up to a special pouch on their mother's body. Inside the pouch, they feed on their mother's milk and drink to keep growing. They live in the pouch for about 280 days and are not ready to live entirely outside it until they are more than a year old.

Wallabies may be cute, but they can be trouble. They sometimes eat farmers' crops and damage pastures where farmers want to graze other animals.

AWK! THEY'D BE SQUISHED!

NAW. THE LITTLE ONE SAYS NO GREEN PIGS HAVE BEEN HERE. LET'S GO.

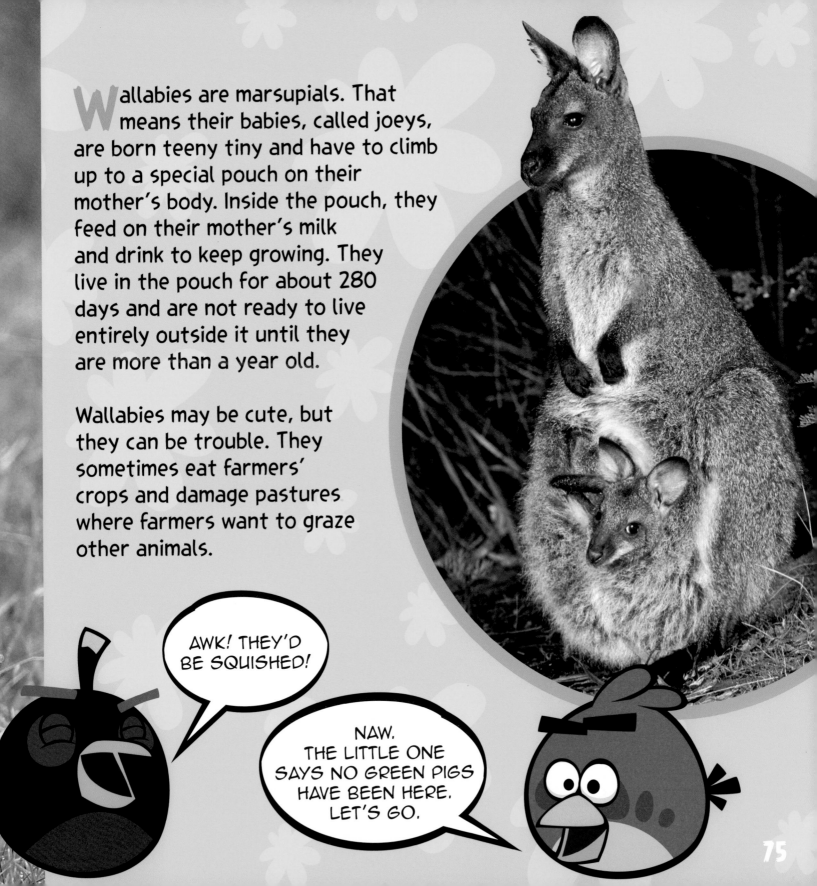

TASMANIAN DEVIL

SIZE: LENGTH: 2.5 FEET (0.8 M), WEIGHT: 9–26 POUNDS (4–12 KG)

ON THE MENU: BIRDS, FISH, FROGS, INSECTS, LIZARDS, SNAKES

SOUNDS LIKE: COUGHS, GROWLS, SNARLS, SCREAMS, SCREECHES; GIVES WARNING SNEEZE BEFORE A FIGHT

FUN FACT: IF A DEVIL IS EATING WELL, ITS TAIL GROWS THICK WITH STORED FAT.

BE CAREFUL. HE LOOKS ANGRY. REALLY ANGRY!

Early settlers to Tasmania saw this animal in action and decided to call it a devil because it is often angry. A Tasmanian devil gets angry if another animal tries to share its food. It doesn't like other animals passing through its territory, either. But guess what? When a devil growls and shows its teeth, it is really just frightened and wants the intruder to leave.

These marsupials usually raise two or three babies. Like wallaby babies, these raisin-sized newborns crawl up into their mother's pouch, and for four months she carries them everywhere.

WHAT'S WRONG WITH ANGRY?

YEAH, WE LIKE ANGRY!

77

MEANWHILE, HIGH OVER AFRICA...

THIS MUST BE TANZANIA.

GOOD. I COULD USE A SNACK.

LOOK, AN ELEPHANT!

GRASSLAND

Tanzania is a country on the continent of Africa. Tanzania is full of grasslands. It has many national parks, where visitors can see some of the most fascinating wildlife on the planet.

Africa

TANZANIA GRASSLAND

AFRICAN ELEPHANT

An elephant's long trunk is a nose. And a noisemaker. And a straw. And a hose. And a hand.

Young elephants, called calves, are raised by their mothers and the other females in their herd. When those adults fear for a calf, they form a circle around the little one to keep it safe.

Elephants make many different sounds to talk to each other. They even have a secret language—rumbles that are so low humans cannot hear them. But other elephants can, even if they are miles away.

SIZE: HEIGHT: UP TO 13 FEET (4 M), WEIGHT: UP TO 14,000 POUNDS (6.4 METRIC TONS)

ON THE MENU: BARK, BRANCHES, FRUIT, GRASSES, LEAVES, ROOTS

SOUNDS LIKE: BARKS, BELLOWS, GROWLS, ROARS, RUMBLES

FUN FACT: AN AFRICAN ELEPHANT'S BIG EARS TELL YOU WHERE IT LIVES. THEY'RE SHAPED LIKE AFRICA.

GIRAFFE

LET'S COUNT THE SPOTS!

Being the world's tallest mammal is great—sometimes. Like when a hungry giraffe can reach leaves nobody else can.

Sometimes it's not so great. Like when a thirsty giraffe needs a drink. Those long legs and neck make getting down to the water tricky. Luckily, giraffes get most of the water they need from the leaves they eat.

A mother giraffe gives birth while standing, so her calf falls to the ground with a *thud.* Half an hour later, the calf is standing. Within a day, it is running with its mother.

80

Lions are often quiet, lying sprawled in the shade together, licking and head rubbing and sharing a purrrrrfectly lazy afternoon. But when lions are loud, their *ro-o-o-oar* can be heard up to five miles (8 km) away.

A family group is called a pride. A pride's females are the hunters. Their job is to keep the pride fed. Males—the ones with large, furry manes—have a job, too: protect their pride. And they do. *Fiercely.*

Cubs stay with their mothers at least two years. Then males wander off to begin their own pride or take over another one. Females stay with their families.

SIZE: LENGTH: 4.5–6.5 FEET (1.4–2 M), PLUS A TAIL UP TO 3.3 FEET (1 M) LONG, WEIGHT: 265–420 POUNDS (120–191 KG)

ON THE MENU: ANTELOPE, BIRDS, BUFFALO, GIRAFFES, IMPALA, RABBITS, REPTILES, WILDEBEESTS, WILD HOGS, ZEBRAS

SOUNDS LIKE: GROWLS, PURRS, ROARS, SNARLS

FUN FACT: WHEN THE PRIDE HAS FRESH MEAT, THE MALES GET TO EAT FIRST, THEN THE FEMALES, AND FINALLY, THE CUBS.

OSTRICH

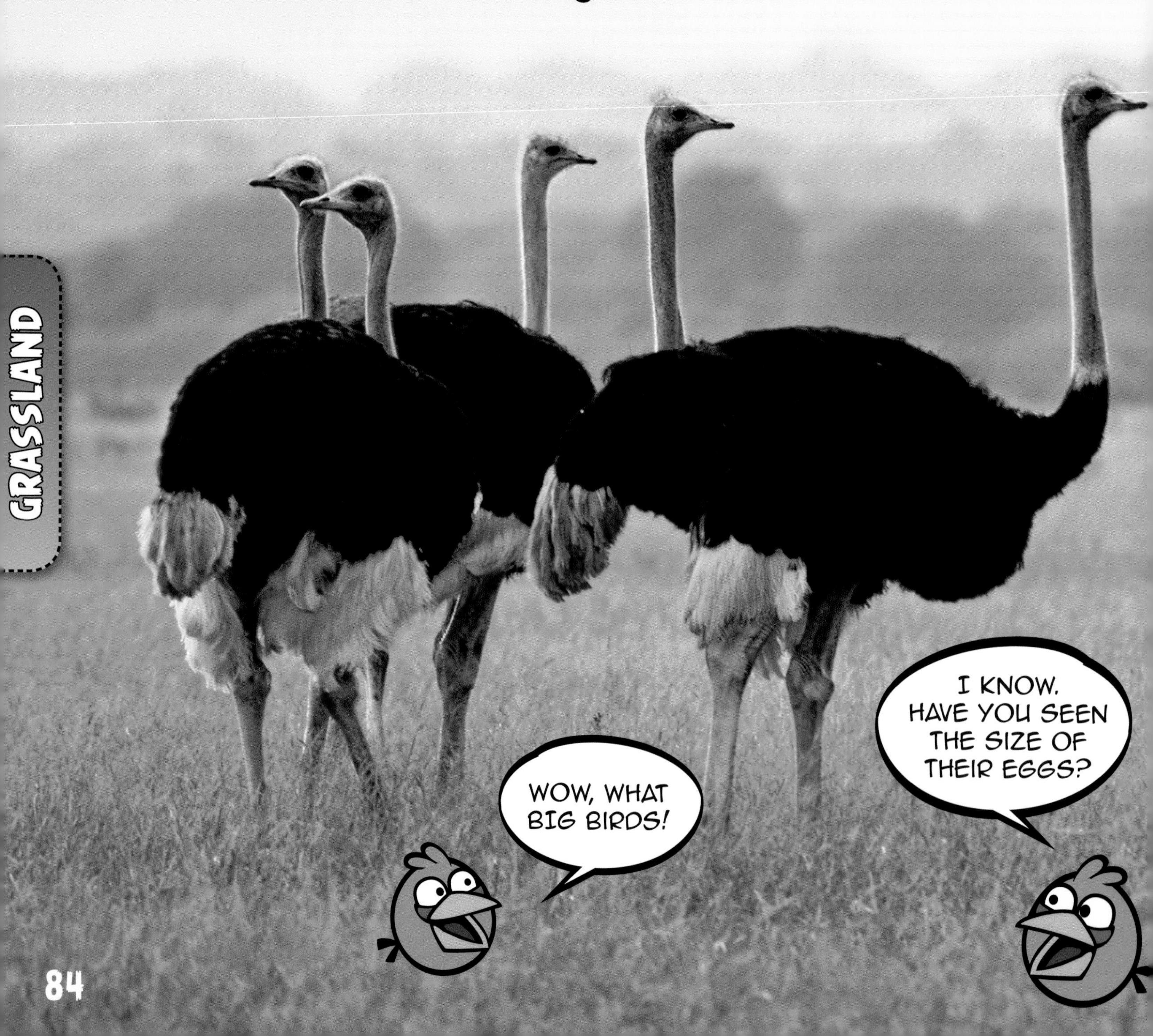

YEP, BIG.
BUT NOT OURS.
LET'S GO!

Ostriches are birds that cannot fly. They probably don't care, though. They have plenty of titles to be proud of: World's Largest Bird. World's Fastest Running Bird. World's Largest Eggs.

Ostriches don't like to fight. When trouble comes, they are likely to run away. Or they might choose to lie low and press their necks to the ground. They think this makes them harder to see.

SIZE: HEIGHT: UP TO 9 FEET (2.7 M), WEIGHT: 140–330 POUNDS (64–150 KG)

ON THE MENU: INSECTS, LIZARDS, PLANTS, ROOTS, SEEDS

SOUNDS LIKE: SNORTS; WHISTLES; LOW, SLOW *WHOO-WHOO-WHOOO*; CHICKS CHIRP AND CHITTER

FUN FACT: WHEN OSTRICH EGGS ARE ABOUT TO HATCH, YOU CAN HEAR THE CHICKS INSIDE. *CHIRP-CHIRP-CHIRP!*

BLACK SWAN

GRASSLAND

These black beauties are smooth swimmers, gliding along gracefully. But when a swan spies a tasty-looking weed under-water—*bloop!*—in goes its head. Seconds later, it resurfaces with lunch.

Cygnets, or baby swans, are covered with fuzzy gray feathers and are able to swim as soon as they hatch.

HE'D BE CUTER IF HE WERE ANGRY.

AHH, WOOK AT THE WITTLE SWANY.

86

SIZE: LENGTH: UP TO 4.7 FEET (1.4 M), INCLUDING NECK, WEIGHT: UP TO 20 POUNDS (9 KG), WINGSPAN: 5.2-6.5 FEET (1.6-2 M)

ON THE MENU: ADULTS: ALGAE, WEEDS JUVENILES: BUGS

SOUNDS LIKE: BUGLES, CROONS, WHISTLES

FUN FACT: IF AN EGG ACCIDENTALLY ROLLS OUT OF THE NEST, SWAN PARENTS USE THEIR NECKS TO ROLL IT BACK IN.

Australia

TASMANIA GRASSLAND

THESE SWANS SAY THE PLATYPUS HAS EGGS! LET'S GO!

PLATYPUS

AWK! THOSE AREN'T OUR EGGS.

SHE SAYS WE COULD ASK THE PENGUINS. THEY ALWAYS HAVE LOTS OF EGGS.

SIZE: LENGTH: 1.5-2 FEET (0.45-0.6 M), INCLUDING TAIL, WEIGHT: UP TO 5.3 POUNDS (3 KG); LARGER IN TASMANIA THAN IN MAINLAND AUSTRALIA

ON THE MENU: INSECTS AND THEIR LARVAE, SHRIMP, TADPOLES

SOUNDS LIKE: CHIRRING GROWL

FUN FACT: PLATYPUS BABIES ARE THE SIZE OF LIMA BEANS.

The platypus could not be more perfectly designed. Its wide, rubbery bill is perfect for scooping insects and worms from muddy river bottoms. Its webbed feet are perfect for swimming. And its beaver-like tail is perfect for steering.

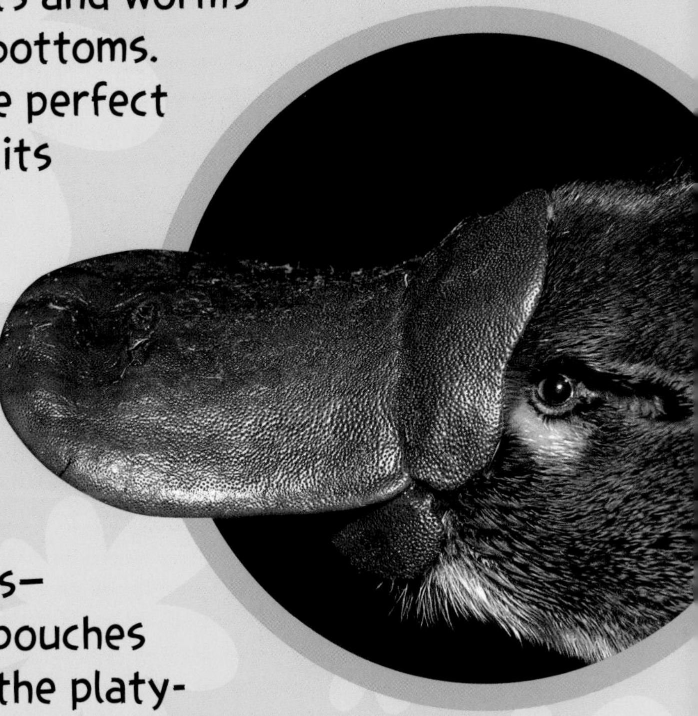

Everything scooped from the mud—including mud and gravel bits—is stored in cheek pouches to be eaten after the platypus swims back to the surface. Those gravel bits come in handy, too. They help the platypus chew its food, since it doesn't have any teeth.

COME ON, BIRDS, LET'S GO!

The platypus is one of only two mammals (the echidna is the other) to lay eggs instead of giving birth to live babies. Platypus eggs are about the size of grapes.

WELCOME TO THE ARCTIC!

THE ARCTIC IS A COLD AREA AT THE TOP, OR NORTHERNMOST, PART OF THE EARTH. THERE IS LOTS OF SNOW IN THE ARCTIC.

UP HERE NEAR THE NORTH POLE, NOBODY ASKS DIRECTIONS.

WHY?

SO WHERE ARE ALL THE PENGUINS?

THE ANSWER IS ALWAYS "SOUTH."

No trees grow on the Arctic tundra, and a portion of this region's ocean remains ice-covered all year long. Countries with land reaching far enough north to be part of the Arctic region are: Canada, Finland, Greenland, Iceland, Norway, Russia, Sweden, and the United States.

POLAR BEAR

> DID YOU ASK HOW TO FIND PENGUINS?

SIZE: HEIGHT: 7-8 FEET (2.1-2.4 M), WEIGHT: UP TO 900–1,600 POUNDS (410-720 KG)

ON THE MENU: FISH, RINGED SEALS, BEARDED SEALS, BIRDS, KELP, WHALE CARCASSES, WALRUSES

SOUNDS LIKE: CHUFFING, GROWLING

FUN FACT: UNDER A POLAR BEAR'S FUR, ITS SKIN IS BLACK, TO BETTER ABSORB THE SUN'S WARMTH.

94

> WE DID, AND HE SAID, "WHAT'S A PENGUIN?"

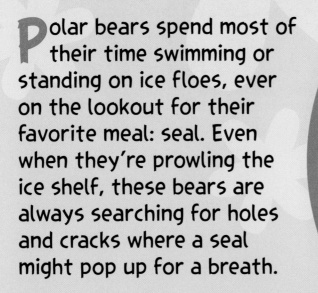

P olar bears spend most of their time swimming or standing on ice floes, ever on the lookout for their favorite meal: seal. Even when they're prowling the ice shelf, these bears are always searching for holes and cracks where a seal might pop up for a breath.

The bottoms of their paws are furry. This makes walking on ice a little warmer and a lot less slippery.

Polar bears dig dens into snowdrifts to get out of the freezing weather or take a rest.

Females give birth in a den, usually to twins. Cubs stay with their mother for more than two years. She teaches them how to survive in the Arctic.

THAT'S W-WEIRD.

KEEP MOVING, BIRDS!

MUSK-OX

SIZE: HEIGHT: 4–5 FEET (1.2–1.5 M), WEIGHT: 500–800 POUNDS (227–363 KG)

ON THE MENU: PLANTS

SOUNDS LIKE: BELLOWS, RUMBLES

FUN FACT: IF A WOLF OR BEAR COMES TOO CLOSE, MUSK-OXEN WILL FORM A TIGHT CIRCLE AROUND THEIR CALVES AND USE THEIR SHARP HORNS TO KEEP THE PREDATOR AWAY.

BRRR, I'M FREEZING.

Musk-oxen look a lot like cattle. Like cattle, they have hooves. Like cattle, they have a four-part stomach. Oh, and they chew cud. What's cud? A chunk of something they swallowed earlier and have thrown back up to chew some more! YUCK!

Unlike their cow cousins, musk-oxen's hair grows almost to their feet. This long hair sheds icy rain and snow and protects the animals from bitter arctic winds.

THINK WE COULD B-BORROW SOME OF THAT LONG HAIR?

97

POLAR

Caribou, also called reindeer, migrate twice each year. As summer nears, herds start north. Hundreds of miles later, they arrive at their summer feeding grounds, where green grasses and plants are plentiful.

After they've grown healthy and strong—and feel winter approaching—they know to head south again so they aren't caught in the harsh northern winters. Their "southern" winter grounds are still very far north, but less cold and snowy.

SIZE: HEIGHT: 4-5 FEET (1.2-1.5 M), WEIGHT: 240-700 POUNDS (109-318 KG)

ON THE MENU: SUMMER: GRASSES AND OTHER PLANTS WINTER: LICHEN, MUSHROOMS

SOUNDS LIKE: SNORTS, GRUNTING ROARS

FUN FACT: ONLY 90 MINUTES AFTER BIRTH, A CARIBOU CALF CAN RUN WITH ITS MOTHER AND KEEP UP WITH THE MIGRATING HERD.

ARCTIC FOX

The arctic fox is another animal with furry paws. Its coat changes color with the seasons—brown in summer and white in winter.

This fox has front-facing ears, which helps it hear so amazingly well that it can make out the faint sounds of its favorite prey—rodents called lemmings—tunneling beneath the snow.

100

SIZE: LENGTH: HEAD AND BODY, 1.5–2.2 FEET (0.5–0.7 M); TAIL, UP TO 1.2 FEET (0.4 M), WEIGHT: 6.5–17 POUNDS (3–8 KG)

ON THE MENU: BERRIES, BIRDS, FISH, LEMMINGS, SQUIRRELS, VOLES, POLAR BEAR LEFTOVERS

SOUNDS LIKE: BARKS, YOWLS, YELPS, WHINES

FUN FACT: WHEN HUNTING IS POOR, ARCTIC FOXES FOLLOW POLAR BEARS, HOPING FOR WHATEVER SCRAPS THE BEAR MIGHT LEAVE BEHIND AFTER A KILL.

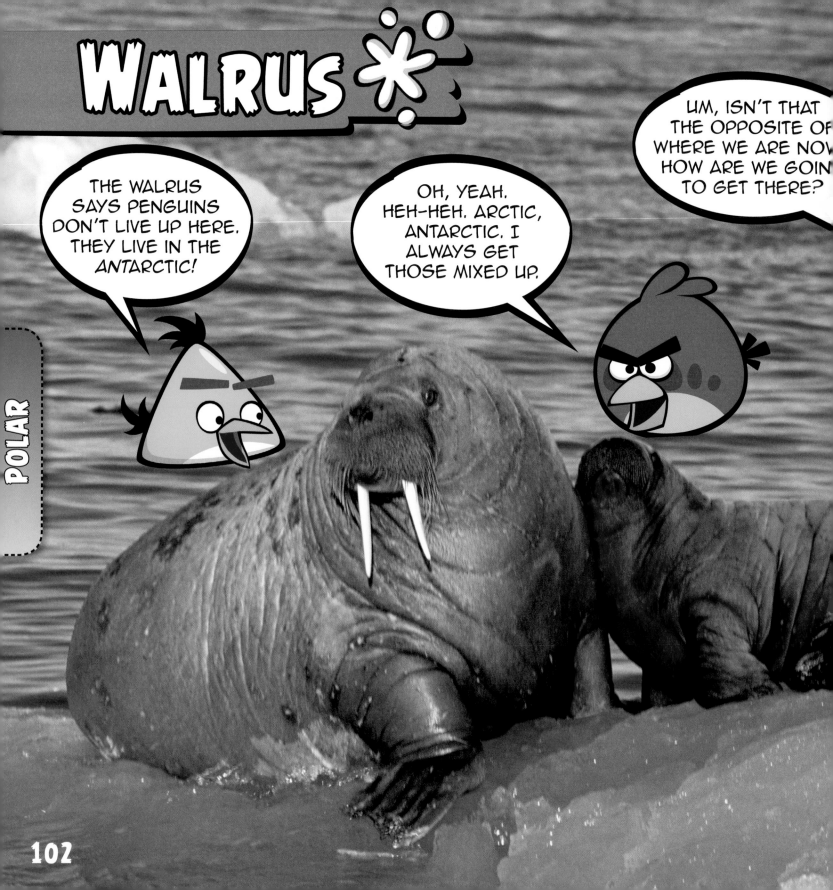

What good is a mustache? If you're a walrus, that mustache finds your lunch. A walrus's favorite foods are clams and mussels, which are only found on the ocean floor. Since it's so dark down there, walruses skim the ocean floor, feeling with their sensitive whiskers for shells.

Those tusks don't just look handsome. A male walrus uses its tusks to help pull his heavy body out of the water. Tusks also break breathing holes through the ice and help show other walruses who's boss.

C'MON, BIRDS! WE'VE GOT AN IDEA!

SIZE: LENGTH: 7.25–11.5 FEET (2.2–3.5 M), WEIGHT: UP TO 1.5 TONS (1.4 METRIC TONS)

ON THE MENU: CLAMS, MUSSELS

SOUNDS LIKE: BARKS, BELLOWS, GRUNTS, GROWLS, MOANS, RUMBLES, SONGS, SPUTTERS, WHISTLES; CAN BLOW "RASPBERRIES"

FUN FACT: BOTH MALE AND FEMALE WALRUSES HAVE TUSKS.

ANGRY BIRDS FLY TO THE SOUTH POLE...

SOUTH POLE

ANTARCTIC

X

WELCOME TO THE ANTARCTIC!

THE ANTARCTIC IS A POLAR AREA AT THE BOTTOM, OR SOUTHERNMOST, PART OF THE EARTH. IT IS OPPOSITE THE ARCTIC REGION.

YEP. THEY'RE BOTH POLAR AREAS.

WHAT'S ALL THIS ICE? IT LOOKS JUST LIKE THE ARCTIC DID.

104

The Antarctic is home to Antarctica, a mountainous, ice-covered, and very windy continent. Not many animals can live here, but the sea is teeming with life. In winter, so much ice forms around the continent's coastlines that it doubles in size.

WANDERING ALBATROSS

No other bird has a wingspan as wide as that of the albatross. Its aerodynamic wings allow an albatross to glide for hours without flapping.

> AN EGG!

An albatross mother lays one egg. She and the father take turns keeping it warm for the two months it takes to hatch. Parents soon leave, returning every three or four days to bring the chick food. Mostly, the big chick sits alone on its nest, through wind and snow and icy storms. After about nine months, it is finally, finally, able to fly. *Whew!*

LEOPARD SEAL

HE SAYS THE PENGUINS HAVE SOME EGGS!

These gigantic seals are named for their black-spotted coats. With their reptile-shaped heads, huge mouths, and sharp teeth, they are fearsome underwater hunters.

They spend most of their time in frigid water, looking for penguins. Like walruses, their bodies have a thick layer of fat, called blubber, which protects them from the cold.

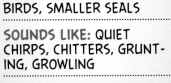

SIZE: LENGTH: 10-11.5 FEET (3-3.5 M), WEIGHT: UP TO 840 POUNDS (380 KG)

ON THE MENU: ADÉLIE (AND OTHER) PENGUINS, CRABS, FISH, OYSTERS, SEA BIRDS, SMALLER SEALS

SOUNDS LIKE: QUIET CHIRPS, CHITTERS, GRUNT-ING, GROWLING

FUN FACT: THE HEAD OF A LEOPARD SEAL IS SHAPED MORE LIKE A REPTILE'S THAN THAT OF OTHER SEALS.

WAIT FOR US!

109

EMPEROR PENGUIN

In this wintry place, where the air can feel unimaginably cold, Emperor penguins huddle for warmth. The middle of the huddle is snug and warm. But the lucky penguins there don't hog the heat. Once they've warmed up, they move to the outside of the group so other, colder penguins can take a turn in the middle.

After the female lays an egg, the male keeps it warm. For two months, he doesn't get a break, not even to eat. He protects that egg atop his feet, covered with his special flap of feathered skin, called a brood pouch.

When the female returns, she takes over the care of the newly hatched chick. Even in a crowd, the mother and chick can recognize each other's voices.

> IF OUR EGGS ARE THAT HUDDL WE'LL NEVE FIND THEM

> WEIRD. THEY SAY NO PIGS HAVE BEEN HERE.

111

WHEW, SOME TRIP!

Along with the Angry Birds, you globe-hopping readers have been to five vastly different habitats—rain forest, desert, ocean, grassland, and polar—and met lots of new animal friends.

How many kinds of eggs did you see along the way?

In the rain forest, there were **insect** eggs belonging to the Blue Morpho butterfly. Those small, green eggs were attached to a leaf. Poison dart frogs, which are **amphibians,** laid their tiny eggs on a leaf, too.

The rain forest was also home to the caiman, a **reptile** whose babies broke out of eggs that couldn't belong to the Angry Birds—they were the wrong shape. There were reptile eggs in the desert, too. You saw the Gila monster's large eggs. And don't forget how the foot-long baby California king snakes slipped and slithered out of their long, narrow shells.

OSTRICH

WELL, WE SURE SAW LOTS OF EGGS.

PLATYPUS

BUT NOT OUR EGGS.

GILA MONSTER

LEATHERBACK SEA TURTLE

CLOWNFISH

EMPEROR PENGUIN

WE'LL TAKE A BREAK, THEN KEEP SEARCHING. HOME, BIRDS!

On a Pacific Ocean beach another reptile, the leatherback sea turtle, buried her eggs in the sand. When the eggs hatched, the baby turtles scurried to the water as fast as their flippers would take them!

You saw tiny clown**fish** eggs in the ocean, floating with the currents as they grew.

While searching the grassland, you found gigantic **bird** eggs. The ostrich chicks inside could chirp even before they hatched. Much smaller were the wandering albatross eggs you saw in their polar habitat. And don't you like the smart way the Emperor penguins keep their precious eggs up off the ice—balanced on their feet?!

The platypus is a **mammal,** yet it lays eggs, too. Australia is the only place it lives. Those little eggs—the size of grapes—held growing baby platypuses just waiting for the right time to hatch.

All those eggs, and none of them belonged to the Angry Birds!

Where did those pesky pigs hide them?

113

115

ANIMAL MAP

USE THIS WORLD MAP TO FIND EACH ANIMAL'S HABITATS.

DESERT

Townsend's big-eared bat
Greater roadrunner
Gila monster
Tarantula
Black-tailed jackrabbit
Desert horned lizard
Burrowing owl
California king snake

RAIN

Jaguar
Harpy eagle
Schneider's dwarf caiman
Poison dart frog
Sloth
Green anaconda
Black-handed spider monkey
Blue Morpho butterfly

OCEAN

Humpback whale
Sea otter
Giant Pacific octopus
Hawaiian monk seal
Great hammerhead shark
Clownfish
Red-footed booby
Leatherback sea turtle

A R

North America

MOJAVE DESERT

Pacific Ocean

Atlantic Ocean

AMAZON RAIN FOREST

South America

A N T

116

Arctic Ocean

I C

POLAR ARCTIC
Polar bear
Musk-ox
Caribou
Arctic fox
Walrus

BONUS ANIMAL! CHINA
Wondering where those cute pandas from our cover are from? They live in the forests of China.

u r o p e

A s i a

PANDA RANGE

Pacific Ocean

GRASSLAND TANZANIA
African elephant
Giraffe
Lion
Ostrich

r i c a

TANZANIA GRASSLAND

Indian Ocean

Australia

GRASSLAND TASMANIA
Red-necked wallaby
Tasmanian devil
Black swan
Platypus

TASMANIA GRASSLAND

POLAR ANTARCTIC
Wandering albatross
Leopard seal
Emperor penguin

Antarctica

C T I C

117

QUIZ TIME!

1. Which of the following animals has the letter "S" in its name?
   a. SEA OTTER
   b. DESERT HORNED LIZARD
   c. HAMMERHEAD SHARK
   d. LEOPARD SEAL
   e. All of the above.

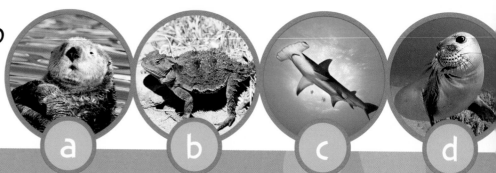

QUIZ TIME!

2. Ostrich eggs, like many other eggs, are oval-shaped. Look around your hou
or playground and identify other things that are shaped like an oval. What ar
some of your favorite oval-shaped things?

PARENT TIP: *Encourage your child to see the shapes "hidden" in objects, such as the triangle of a pizza slice or the rectangle of a house.*

3. The pigs have stolen some of the letters from the names of these desert animals. Can you figure out what letters are missing?

   a. B U R R O W I N G O _ L

   b. B L A C K - T A I L E D J A C K R A _ B I T

   c. T A R A N _ U L A

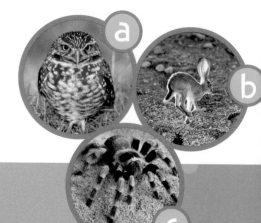

118

4. These black-handed spider monkeys are swinging their way through the rain forest. They love to jump around and play with their friends. What else do you think these monkeys are up to? Grab a piece of paper and write a story about what else these monkeys will do today.

5. Here is a list of a few of the animals we met in the Pacific Ocean. Take a piece of paper and practice writing these animal names on your own!

OTTER, SEAL, CLOWNFISH, OCTOPUS

6. Unscramble these words to find some rain forest-related words.

a. TWE   b. SEETR   c. NPAOCY   d. MAZONA

__ __ __   __ __ __ __ __   __ __ __ __ __ __   __ __ __ __ __ __

7. You probably see a lot of animals as you travel around, too. Keep a travel log and write down the names of the animals that you run across.

PARENT TIP: Have your child carry a little notebook on excursions to write down what he sees, even if it's nothing but scribbles.

8. The hammerhead shark has quite the face profile! Use your finger to trace the outline of the hammerhead shark.

9. Say the name of the animal in the main picture. Listen to the beginning sound. Then, say the name of each animal shown in the other pictures. Pick which animal has the same beginning sound as the animal in the main picture.

a

b

c

PARENT TIP: Have your child draw a picture of an animal. Then help her identify the first letter of the animal pictured and write it.

10. On a piece of paper, draw a picture of a lion like the ones that live in Tanzania, as shown on page 82. Then, color the body yellow, the mane orange, and the ears pink.

BONUS ACTIVITIES

The best way to see a variety of wildlife from around the world is to visit a zoo. But you can have animal fun at home, too. Here are additional activities you and your child can share to take the experiences beyond the pages of this book.

TREASURE HUNT
(COOPERATION)

As a caiman marches along, it keeps its head up, searching for clues that will lead to its next meal. Have your child search for clues by hosting a treasure hunt. Invite a couple of her friends over. Before they arrive, hide a treasure somewhere outdoors or around the house. Write simple clues on small scraps of paper and hide them too. (For example: You'll find the next clue under something that's blue.) Each clue should lead to another, until the children are finally led to the treasure. The treasure should be something they can share: a snack, a slip of paper announcing a trip to a playground (or zoo!), or art supplies.

THE ART OF CAMOUFLAGE
(ART)

A poison dart frog's colorful skin warns predators away. On printer or construction paper, draw other animals from the book with your child and color them with wild colors and patterns. Discuss why it's important for some animals to be brightly colored and for others to blend in with their surroundings.

SLOTH CRAWL
(EXERCISE)

Sloths are strong, if slow, climbers. But on the ground, they have a tough time getting around because their hind legs are weak. Have your child lie on the floor and be a sloth, dragging himself forward using only his arms.

SING A SONG
(COMMUNICATION)

Humpback whales communicate with many different sounds. What if you could only communicate with sounds other than words? Would one *bloop* mean "Let's take a walk"? How would you ask for a drink of water? Try communicating only with sounds—*bloops*, grunts, growls, mews, smacks, tongue clicks, purrs, or anything but words—for one hour.

GROW A FLOWER
(GARDENING)

Butterflies sip flower nectar. See what kinds of butterflies you can attract by planting some flowers. A few butterfly favorites are butterfly bushes, black-eyed susans, marigolds, and purple coneflowers. If you want to grow flowers from seed, try colorful zinnias. Plant them in soil-filled egg cartons and place them near a sunny window. Keep them watered and growing until it's warm enough to transplant them outdoors.

NIGHT WATCH
(OBSERVING)

Bats, owls, and many other predators hunt at night. What is different about night besides the lack of light? Sit outside with your child as night falls and observe the changes that take place. What sounds do you hear? Does the air feel warmer or cooler? Do colors change as the sun goes down? Do you see flying insects? Bats? Discuss which animals hunt at night and why.

FOUR-FINGERED FUN
(DEXTERITY)

Black-handed spider monkeys have only four fingers (no thumbs). With your child, try taping your thumbs to your palms. With your four remaining fingers, can you pick up a penny? A paper plate? Can you eat using a spoon? Color with a crayon?

PLAY A GAME
(FOLLOWING DIRECTIONS)

When being chased by a predator, jackrabbits run in a zigzag pattern. Play a game that lets you move like the animals in this book (for example, Mother, May I?). First, write these animal names on eight index cards: frog, elephant, jackrabbit, roadrunner, snake, tarantula, polar bear, penguin. Players line up on one side of a yard or playground, and a leader stands on the other. The leader pulls an animal card from the stack in his hand and asks one player at a time to move forward a certain number of steps, moving like that animal. The first one to reach the leader becomes the next leader.

FEEL YOUR WAY
(DEDUCTION)

An octopus reaches into dark places and feels with its sensitive suckers. Place a number of common small objects into a paper bag. Have your child reach inside and see how many of the objects she can identify by feel. If she gets stuck, have her ask about the object's properties—size, shape, texture—to make identification easier.

BUILD A BOAT
(RECYCLING CRAFT)

Sea otters spend much of their lives floating. Try creating something else that floats—a boat. You'll need a clean top or bottom half of a small plastic or Styrofoam food container (boat body), a craft stick or plastic straw (mast), and colorful shapes cut from an old magazine. Use masking tape to make the stick or straw stand straight in the center of your boat. Tape a triangle to the mast. Try out your boat in a kiddie pool or bathtub. What makes the boat move? What makes the strongest wind, blowing at the sail or fanning it with a large piece of cardboard? Try different mast/sail designs—whatever floats your boat!

JUMPING FINGER
(OBSERVING)

A hammerhead shark's eyes are far apart and work together to help it see very well. Human eyes work together, too. But just because ours are closer together doesn't mean they're seeing exactly the same thing. Here's how you can prove it. Look at something across a room: a picture, a clock, a light switch. Close one eye, then hold up a finger in front of you, moving it until it's blocking the object. Now without moving your finger, close the opened eye and open the closed eye. Did your finger jump from the object?

READ AROUND THE WORLD
(READING)

Red-footed booby parents keep their egg warm with their feet—for 46 days! Too bad they don't have books, like humans, to make the waiting more interesting. Take your child to the library and find books about a favorite animal that lives somewhere far away. Read all about it. Discuss whether or not this animal could be a family pet. Why or why not?

HOPSCOTCH ADDITION
(MATH)

Wallabies are quite the hoppers. How about combining hopping with math? With sidewalk chalk, draw boxes on a driveway or sidewalk to look like basic calculator keys ("0" at the bottom, and, along the side, remember the +, −, and =). The first player gently tosses a stone into the 1 square, then hops on "keys" that, added together, equal 1: 1 + 0 = 1. Then the same player tosses a stone onto the 2 and tries for that equation. If he steps on a line or answers incorrectly, the next player gets a turn. The first player to make it to 9 is the winner.

SCRAP IT
(TELLING A STORY)

African elephant families stick together, traveling many miles as they look for food. The next time you and your child take a trip together, take plenty of pictures and help her note her favorite experiences or anything that made the trip special for her. When you return home, help her make a scrapbook of the trip, then pull it out from time to time and let her tell you or other relatives her vacation story.

COLORFUL WORLD
(ART)

Nature gives polar bears white coats so they blend into their wintry surroundings. But nature isn't stingy with colors. Go on a nature hike, bringing with you a color wheel you've printed out (Google "simple color wheel"). Using the color wheel as a guide, gather a variety of colorful objects from nature, such as feathers, flowers, grasses, leaves, and rocks, and put them into a bag to take home. Then create a Nature's Color Wheel collage by gluing your items onto a large sheet of paper, color by color.

REPEAT AFTER ME
(COMMUNICATION)

A lion's roar can be heard five miles (8 km) away. It's much easier to hear somebody right behind you...or is it? For this game you'll need paper and pencils, markers, or crayons. Sit back to back with your child. Have him draw a picture. But as he's drawing, he must tell you everything he's doing—which color he's using, what shape he's drawing, and so on. You follow his instructions (no clarifying questions allowed) to draw your own matching picture. When he's finished, see if your drawings look anything alike. Now try the same exercise, but you do the primary drawing and see if you can give clear enough instructions that he draws the same picture as you do.

CLOUD ZOO
(OBSERVING)

Giraffes have a very distinctive shape. It's those long necks! Lie on a blanket with your child. Relax and watch the clouds. What animal shapes can you identify as they float by?

X MARKS THE SPOT
(MAPMAKING)

Twice each year, caribou herds migrate hundreds of miles, guided by an internal compass. Most humans don't have internal compasses, but we do have maps, which are fun to follow and to create. Walk around your neighborhood, then draw a simple map from your house or apartment to various points of interest: a mailbox, a restaurant, a certain tree, a park, a favorite neighbor's place. You might even try mapping your yard, counting the footsteps to a garage or swing set or hydrant. Proportions don't have to be perfect.

GLOSSARY

Not sure what all those big words mean?
Check out the definitions of some of the harder words right here.

ACROBATIC
Skilled at balance and moving quickly and easily

AERODYNAMIC
Having a shape that makes an animal or object move easier through the air or water

BURROW
A hole or tunnel dug by an animal

CAPYBARA
A mammal that looks like a giant guinea pig

CHRYSALIS
A hard outer case covering a butterfly or moth in its pupa stage

CHUFFING
A regular, sharp puffing sound

DEN
An animal's resting place, hidden from others

ECHIDNA
Long-snouted, spiny mammal that lives in Australia and New Guinea

FLOES
Sheets of floating ice

FLUKE
The tail fin of a whale

FRIGID
Very, very cold

GRAVEL
Small stones broken from bigger rocks or worn by water

HABITAT
The natural home of an animal or plant

HIBERNATING
Spending the winter in a deep sleep

INTRUDER
Animal (or person) that comes into another's space

KELP
A tough seaweed with long, striped leaves

LICHEN
Slow-growing plants that grow in crusty patches, or bushy growths on tree trunks, rocks, or bare ground

POLE
Either of the two locations (North Pole or South Pole) on the surface of the Earth that are the northern and southern ends of the axis of rotation

PRECIPITATION
Rain, snow, sleet, or hail that falls to the ground

PREDATOR
An animal that hunts another

PREY
An animal that is hunted by another for food

RODENTS
Gnawing mammals like hamsters, guinea pigs, mice, porcupines, rats, and squirrels

SENSES
Sight, smell, hearing, taste, and touch

STINGRAYS
Flat, diamond-shaped fish that spend most of their time on the ocean floor

TERRITORY
Area of land

TUNDRA
Area of land where the ground is permanently frozen

VENOMOUS
Having venom, or poison, and able to inject the venom by stinging or biting

VOLE
A small, typically burrowing, mouselike rodent

INDEX

Boldface indicates illustrations.

PHOTO CREDITS

Published by the National Geographic Society
John M. Fahey, Jr., Chairman of the Board and Chief Executive Officer
Timothy T. Kelly, President
Declan Moore, Executive Vice President; President, Publishing and Digital Media
Melina Gerosa Bellows, Executive Vice President; Chief Creative Officer, Books, Kids, and Family
Sanna Lukander, Vice President of Book Publishing, Rovio

Prepared by the Book Division
Hector Sierra, Senior Vice President and General Manager
Nancy Laties Feresten, Senior Vice President, Kids Publishing and Media
Jonathan Halling, Design Director, Books and Children's Publishing
Jay Sumner, Director of Photography, Children's Publishing
Jennifer Emmett, Vice President, Editorial Director, Children's Books
Eva Absher-Schantz, Design Director, Kids Publishing and Media
Carl Mehler, Director of Maps
R. Gary Colbert, Production Director
Jennifer A. Thornton, Director of Managing Editorial

Staff for This Book
Jan Schulte-Tigges, Art Director
Pasi Pitkänen, Graphic Designer & Illustrator
Laura Nevanlinna, Content Manager
Maria Mikkonen, Sales Coordinator
Mari Elomäki, Project Editor
Susan Kehnemui Donnelly, Project Editor
Nicole Lazarus, Designer
Lori Epstein, Senior Illustrations Editor
Miriam Stein, Photo Editor
Hillary Moloney, Illustrations Assistant
Rebecca Baines, Editor
Dan Sipple, Illustrator
Grace Hill, Associate Managing Editor
Joan Gossett, Production Editor
Lewis R. Bassford, Production Manager
Susan Borke, Legal and Business Affairs

Manufacturing and Quality Management
Phillip L. Schlosser, Senior Vice President
Chris Brown, Vice President, NG Book Manufacturing
George Bounelis, Vice President, Production Services
Nicole Elliott, Manager
Rachel Faulise, Manager
Robert L. Barr, Manager